Penny Ante Feud 17
On the way way way down

Penny Ante Feud 17: On the way way way down is published by Shoe Music Press, Alpharetta, GA USA. Its contents are protected by copyright law where applicable.

Cover image: *Our Political Landscape* by Ed Markowski

Penny Ante Feud has appeared in serial under ISSN: 2153-6422.

Email us at shoemusicpress@gmail.com and visit us online at www.shoemusicpress.com

BZ Niditch

In the Big Apple

In a spurt of light
my sax waits for me
wishing to be part
of a new world
jazz symphony,
like any fresh violet
snuggling up
from the earth
already missing
Andy and Edie
from the Factory
whose gates
have closed,
wanting to again
believe in art
and not commercials,
to be undisturbed
on a wall
full of my city's graffiti
by a back alley
in the Big Apple
on a a wintry dog day
I'm driving in my taxi
blowing sax riffs
as rain showers

like dusty shadows
fall on the windshield
and in my poncho
I lost at L.A.X.
fed up with no energy
left in my travel,
my head stuck down
from the cops
in traffic lanes
of so many hours
with uneasy streets
picking up my friend
by a dark doorway
of the club
with dying flowers
intoxicated by the night.

henry 7. reneau, jr.

[i ~ me] + mine ≡ [they ~ them] = us

> it was us.
> it was us all along.
> the *they*
> we labeled *them*
> indivisible
> in *our* ignorance
> the focus of
> *their* governing
> is cause & effect
> that is *us*.

Note:

~ equivalent; similar

≡ is equivalent—used in statements to show how much of one substance will react with a given quantity of another so as to leave no excess of either (is identical to)

Carla Ronk

hemorrhaging

the cut starts the bleed
like everything else, it is by design
the risk you take is never knowing how deep you have gone
always hoping it will be deep enough to bring on the deep sleep so longed for

it's our secret, we master the art of disguise
no one knows because they keep their eyes closed
but we like it that way so we can bleed as we go
once interrupted it angers me so

why do you do this a stranger asks
i steal from the old song, we bleed to know we are alive
but the pain is staggering, it takes my breath away
you want it to hurry and bleed itself out,
so the sleep you long for can finally come about

then they say no do not go
which rings empty, so void of sincerity
it sickens me and i force them away
the solitude is bliss, these interruptions are merely an insult

i wait for the outcome never knowing when it might stop
some days I want it to end, some days I want to rush it to bring sleep
which is more welcome, sleep or relief
both seem better than the pressure of bricks on my chest
so I wait for I do not know what else to do

Dan Von Der Embse

Confession

Bless me father I confess
to breaking every one
of your ten commandments
except the one *thou shalt not kill*

But still I killed in crueler ways
through love I choked, drowned
shot in cold blood before it ever
had a chance to breathe

Bless me father I forget
it has been so long since
my last confession I have
no more memory of sin

Note: Sadly we learned of Dan's passing in February of this year. Our condolences go out to his family and loved ones.

Ag Synclair

Eleventh-Hour

I don't expect dancing
with such ample feet

or even a small
intangible offering

like peeling away
the hard skin

from every tangled thing
that should be turned

inside out, exposed to the
teeth of disagreeable air

all its little puzzles
raining down on us, the trees.

Julie Finch

Homecoming

It's December, and 80 degrees in Houston.
In Philadelphia, where my oldest brother lives,
the snow is clinging to the myriad colored leaves
as he boards a plane for home.
He is coming to spend the winter, and look
after my aging parents, who, together, live alone.
The sun, though warm, is weakened here now
in Texas, filtered through the daylight savings we've
all grown accustomed to, an ode to shorter days.
Everything seems to go faster now.
Weeks go by in a blur; it doesn't make sense.
Even the seasons, which do not stand on ceremony
here, collide and coincide with each other in
a blaze, a comet, a maddening mix of the air
conditioning one day, heat the next.
It is Houston as it's always been,
though everything is changing, everywhere.
Even as it grows, my city, my life is shrinking,
or soon to be. What can you do but make the
most of every minute, knowing there will come a
day when one more face, one more life has
slipped away, and time, no longer on your side,
has become something of an enemy.
Time taunts with its heritage of grief, to each of us
it comes: to my brother, who will arrange my

parents' many medications into tiny boxes marked
Monday through Sunday.
He will make their coffee in the morning, and slowly,
carefully drink his own.
He will cook for them the meals his mother is
unwilling to at last, after 81 years, she can't handle
the stove; she is tired. So tired.
He will sit with my father who rarely leaves the house,
side by side in adjacent chairs and watch a television
turned up unnervingly loud, and he will bear it.
He will wear shorts in winter here, and Crocs, and
decide that after so long of loathing his roots, the
humidity, the crass and obscenely concrete bland
banks of strip malls, the rednecks and oil & gas snobs,
he is, in fact, home, relieved to be here in the sun,
however long it may last.

Amit Parmessur

POEM: Demonic Mantra

I want to suck on an erect cigarette,
and let the smoke make love with my tongue.

I want to swallow some foamy beer and
let it turn my veins into violent whips.

I want to dig that juicy oyster,
and drink its elixir from a silvered chalice.

I want to climb, to caress virgin hills and
let them bruise my belly.

I want to charm that one singing mermaid
into the colors of my lustful heart.

I want.

I want to.

Want.

I want to be sucked into that virgin
oyster and be a saint

again and again
and let myself rape the smoke,
singing to be or to be
there'll be no question.

Rob O'Keefe

If I Knew

What you say
is not what I hear,
the gravity of your words
pulls at their meaning,
bending, distorting
some parabola of purpose
that extends beyond
this room, this existence.

Your lifetime of words
comes to rest
on another world,
where a race yet to be born
will study the echoes
of your syllables,
and comprehend everything –
except you.

While I, long gone,
will ask the ghosts
if they understood
your remnant forms,
why the time and
space between us
became such a vast expanse,
when neither of us moved.

Simon Perchik

Inside Every Flower

Just a toy though the string
is still afraid, tied as if inside
a weightlessness is pulling it
closer and closer and can't let go
caged in on all sides
by the color blue and emptiness

—a trapped balloon, banded
the way all buoys spread out
and the channel lurking below
unravels as rain that has no water yet

—it's always been like this
at carnivals, balloons by the hundreds
coming from a single fountain
that never falls back

—you can't take in enough air
—your arms leak and you drown
in the overcast that has no shadow yet
not yet touching down in the cry
from your hands over your heart.

*

You pick away at the Earth
as if your grave was filled
with the wait for flowers: one foot

already pleased, the other
still wrapped in dirt
weighed down stone by stone

the way fruit is ripened
keyed up and seaworthy, is lowered
into a wooden box

that never leaves shore
just the loading and unloading
though step by step

you overflow from a single rock
broken into twigs
coming by for your mouth

—you want to walk out, trade
make a deal tit for tat
the dry grass that has no blossoms yet.

*

Night after night a paper cup
filled with hillside
and the makeshift thirst

that won't move an inch
keeps damp in an invisible mouth
where oceans are buried

—there's no place to want
—there's only take-out and the lid
is already closed

though it leaves some room
to lift the shoreline to your lips
—this coffee is flowing

from a darkness suddenly homesick
though you don't hear the mourners
or the grass splash over one hand

and with the other you open the cup
just to see what's inside
as if black still counts for something.

*

You hold the phone
the way all wounds begin
then tell you the worst

how their familiar drone
has to be cared for
kept forever under your heart

broken down into the night sky
—what you grip
is the unrelenting hum

longing for more room
for lift, closer
—it's not going to happen

—you need more time
so the bare wires
that once could fit into your hand

become silent again
and you are drifting
on a cold, clear day

left off the hook
as the cry
that turns into a chained animal.

*

As if each wave was being pardoned
sent off the way the moon
was covered with these flowers
and harvests that even today
are just hours apart
allowed to leave

—-the first turbulence on Earth
remembered vaguely as moonlight
that still needs to be held down
soothed, at first with dirt
then evenings, then stones
and the gentle splash
on its way to the bottom

—-an ancient rage! what was spared
is this thirst for her eyelids
between your lips --the same undertow
inside every flower
closer and closer and in your arms
the sea who has forgotten everything
to get away with it.

Colin James

An Anemic Dynamic

Gray is not her color,
orange symbolically unjust.
Aquamarineish is oky doky.
I saw you before anyone else,
Sanctus Espiritus.
lurking too tall by half.
Bend and the bush will crush dust,
enough to create a diversion
or a religion.

J. J. Steinfeld

Conversational

How much more interesting
at staid dinner parties
conversation for the sake
of conversation
is the gregarious and scarred woman
who jabs a salad fork
into the table and explains
that when she was twelve
the Ferris wheel malfunctioned
and she was stuck for nearly an hour
in a compartment with an uncle
who family rumour had it
had been to jail three times
for crimes that seemed ambiguous.

How much more interesting
while standing in line
fearful and depressed
and waiting for inoculation
for a recently discovered disease
to be either in front of or behind
the talkative man
who touches himself where
his gregarious wife has scars
and explains she is now

at a dinner party with a man
he will call later
and threaten with something
stronger than a recently
discovered disease.

Nathan Blan

Weekly Bath

Beams of light
from what I do not know
as white as the old man's skin
when I have him undressed
to wash him
the beams coming through the window
to the right of our bed
they look so solid I am thankful
I have no hanging pictures
that could be knocked to the floor
as the lights explore the wall
and wake the old man
only half an hour after
I got him to sleep

and I think
what if the lights are from Martians
or men from the Moon
though it would make me
even less of a man I would scream
yes I think I would scream
if I saw green faces
at the window

now I am afraid to look
towards the window
afraid that I will see
green faces close to the glass
so afraid that I move closer
to the old man
and hide my face against the back
of his sleeping body
though there are still
two days to go
until I wash him again
and he stinks to high heaven

Star McGill

Had I Known

Don't fear the darkness that claws at your heels,
whose vapor winds around just behind you,
oh, I know the nights of no end,
the on your hands and knees,
wailing, body rocking back and forth,
working to expel the sadness and fear that
has flooded into every fingertip and down into each toe,
until your heart and lungs are drowning,
gasping, from the endless hollow,
I know you will claw the bed as you douse it with tears,
those are magic tears my dear one,
because from them you will arise,
not who they think you are,
not who you think you should be
you will arise, you will arise,
you,
don't recoil from it,
swallow it up,
if you don't experience those tears,
dear one, you will never be you,
feel them,
and when they have wrung from you
every drop of water that forms you,
every tide that push-pulls you,
having resolved to survive,

having arrived at the truth that wills your heart to beat,
arise and unfold to your highest height,
stretch one foot solidly in front of the other,
every step walking out of your old skin
letting it fall away as an offering to appease the darkness,
every step more golden and strong,
and your legs pillars,
rock hard and powerful to carry you through,
my dear one, slice yourself on this world
and open wide,
showing to the sky, to the moon, to the sun
the threads that make you whole

Jennifer Wesle

Ninety nine percent present—
let not the revolution die.

I.

We have no hope but to unite in love:
The 6th great extinction isn't imminent
It has already begun and we are paralyzed.
We've emerged into adulthood
As the passive generation.
We have the hipsters
A whole subculture lacking true direction
Devoid of true connection
Entirely superficial—entirely for fashion.
The beats/hippies had their fallout shelter
Paranoid Parents, Russian enemy, Cold war doldrums
But the beats beat the system
Grew beards and hitchhiked
MAD across America. Sharing love
Be-ins love-ins sit-ins flower power.
We are clutching the means of our destruction
With bloodstained hands
Oil—money—petroleum—plastic—money
As though it were savior—as though we are not slaves.
Remember when we were innocent?
Babies' heads smelled like promise
Like hope and a milk breakfast.

Now we have Ukraine protesters killed like cattle
Olympics strategically at the big bad next door neighbour.
Remember when we were young?
We slid on garbage bags down snow banks
And ate brunch on sunny January mornings.
Sometimes I wish I were the new beat generation
Then I could be heard thru my words
My voice would be my weapon and my rose,
I could make love to my whole country
Create the greatest hand-in-hand chain of solidarity
But I am logged in—I am staring at this screen
And clicking the same app
And posting my life away
One update at a time.

II.

Look! I want to be a human being—a being present in person
Now I want to laugh in circles on the floor
Now I want jam sessions in the basement
Now I begin a project to unite us
To find the shoulders rubbing
The sacred silence.
Now I will visit New York
Sit on a corner in Greenwich Village
Find the ghosts of Kerouac and Corso
We'll drink at the Whitehorse Tavern (567 Hudson Street)
I will solve this whole mess over beers
I am sure of it.

Look! I want to be a human being—more than a soldier for the system
I see a debauchery—this corruption paints our perspectives
The media has fed us the *Image of Us*
Being atop the mountains of materialism
Burning bills upon a golden grill
Glowing face of Her Majesty
Illuminating ruby faces
Ecstatic under static star filled heavens of a Christian God
Ecstatic amidst the snoring symphonies of popular taste
Ecstatic underneath measles infected complementary woolen blankets
Ecstatic under watchful eye of Big Brother security.

But, we are not ecstatic, we are home alone
Staring at humming screens of bluelight silence
Slowly collapsing into ourselves
And once we dreamt of sweet surf mornings
And once we dreamt of rooftop paradise parties in Tarifa
And once we dreamt of our clan of sisters
And once we dreamt of clean air and water
And once we dreamt of Peace on Earth
And once we dreamt of Nineteen Ninety Two.

III.

Where is our hope?
I have bathed myself
Baptized in holy rivers
Peripatetic to understand Buddha
I have cleansed my soul on the Camino

I have drank the Kool-Aid
I have read Nietzsche, Twain and Dr. Seuss
I have eaten the fungi
I have sang sutras from the highest order
Read tarot in the foothills of Banff
And I still cannot find what is proper
And I still cannot seem to find God.
I've been quoting di Prima, Dylan, Thompson,
Sitting on the courthouse steps
I've been contemplating with this quart of Whiskey
Naked but for this carnival mask.

OH!

Malkovich. Malkovich. Malkovich.
The lies they tell us
And all we do is tag and repost.
I am done with your economic excuses
I am done with your disposable love
I am done with your fifteen seconds of you-tube fame
I will cut off my ear
      Just like he did
So that I cannot hear the plastic auto-tuned opera.

IV.

You with ten dollars and twenty-five cents per hour
You with illuminated prosperity

In front of a backdrop of junkies
You throwing matches at me while I'm walking
Driving by in gasoline powered V8 motors
You who washed our hands with turpentine
You who cleansed your souls with paycheques
You who cheered at Euro unity
You who rode the metro smiling
You who then graduated to town cars
Quickly followed by the paparazzi
You who laughed when we were drowning
In the unforgiving sea of silence
You who started wars of petroleum
You who did not value working class
You who perpetuated ignorance
    Hoorah to red scarved communists!
    Auguri to the brave ones!
I have filled my tank with hand outs
I have replenished my tomatoes
I have drawn the lines out on the concrete
I have the guidebooks to revolution
I, the ones who see the hope still
With eyes red from never sleeping
With mouths open to the raindrops
With ears shaped like sea-shells
Howling with the full-moon high-tide
Give us bread or let us sleep now
And our armies of peaceful protest
Will wake up tomorrow morning
And rise like phoenix from the ashes

And we'll coalesce with the masses
And our guns will fire peonies
And our soldiers will hand out poems
And everyone will lift their faces
And turn into doves under the sun.

Alan Catlin

So it Goes

Unable to sleep in the heat,
the words dead on the page
before they are written down.
The fetid, still Summer air
outside this two bit room,
outside this won't-open grime
stained window. The useless,
rusting fire escape barely pinned
to the tenement more likely to
fall than to hold weight.
The stale smell of cigarettes
and smoldering butts in the
overflowing ash tray.
Down in the street, you can
hear them, the living dead
drunks outside the Last Drop
bar, "You bitch. You stupid,
useless bitch. You spilled last
call….." Nothing open now
but graves ten foot deep and
waiting to be filled.
"Shut up down there or a drink
isn't all that's going to be spilled."
"Eat shit and die, asshole."
And so it goes. All night, every night.

Dead white man music through
the static on the radio. Three bottles
of red wine down. Two to go.

Leslie Philibert

Rented Sky

Star to let
to a cat-lover
and friend of

less perfect dahlias,
to putter-outers of
unwashed milk bottles,

to curtain shifters
and spectacle sinkers
to all those gods

of Victoria`s terraces
all waiting for
the flat upstairs.

Ed Markowski

For Beatrice From Buffalo

In the midst of a record setting blizzard the red words that made
her poem a poem became entirely silent as I fell deeper and deeper into the snow white heat of her lips.

New to Penny Ante Feud? Catch up on our back issues:

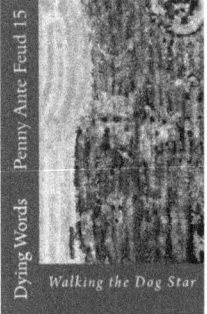
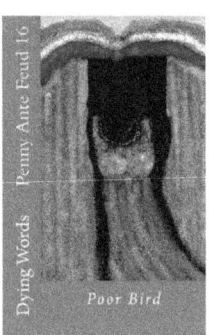

Please check our website www.shoemusicpress.com for current pricing (special bulk discount and author pricing available).

www.ingramcontent.com/pod-product-compliance
Lightning Source LLC
Chambersburg PA
CBHW031508040426
42444CB00007B/1251